Holding
The Border

Holding The Border

Words From The Working Week

A collection of poems

by

DR JAMES BROCKBANK

THE CHOIR PRESS

Copyright © 2025 Dr James Brockbank

All rights reserved. No part of this publication may be reproduced or transmitted in any form or by any means, electronic or mechanical including photocopying, recording or any information storage or retrieval system, without prior permission in writing from the publishers.

The right of Dr James Brockbank to be identified as the author of this work has been asserted by him in accordance with the Copyright, Designs and Patents Act 1988

First published in the United Kingdom in 2025 by
The Choir Press

ISBN 978-1-78963-515-7

Doctors enter the complex narratives of illness and have to imagine what the situation must be like from the inside ... to do so requires in addition to imagination, a fluency as reader and receiver of accounts of others that is not taught in medical school ... clinical work often depends on this capacity of a doctor to intuit or envision the patient's situation.

(Dr Rita Charon, 2011)

In memory of

Emmie, David and Rick

Contents

With Thanks	ix
Introduction	x
The Consulting Room	1
Life Force	2
Manifesto	3
Content	4
The Now and Then	5
Lifeline	6
No Tomorrow	7
Rooted in duty	8
A drink at lunchtime	9
If you are listening	10
The Sound of Life	11
Courageous	12
Duty Man	13
So You Want To Be a GP	14
Illusion	16
The Final Question	18
The Court Report	19
Castaway	20
Face	22
Walter	23
"I'm Just Nipping Out to the Post Office"	24
The Cake	25
Homemade Biscuits and Rhubard	26
The Circle of Life	27

As Death Came In	28
"Can you come over doc"	30
Travel Companion	31
A World Apart	32
Heroes	33
The Last Cigarette	34
He walked into the garage	35
The Computer is King	36
When the Mad House Beckoned	38
Unseeing Undone	39
A Walk in the Park	40
Words From The Working Week	41
The Clean Whipping	42
Conversations	43
Strung Out	44
If it was my child	45
Falling Into Darkness	46
The Domestic Zoo	47
Touch	48
The Whipping Boy	49
Again, Again and Again	50
Letting go	51
Unmasked And Set Free	52
Under the weather	54

With Thanks

I am indebted to the many patients who in times of sickness, uncertainty, and sometimes in crisis, came through the door and revealed their stories, they taught me what it means to be a GP.

I'm also grateful to the many colleagues and friends who over the years were supportive when I needed them, especially my partners at the Practice. It was their gift of a residential writing course, where I was encouraged to write poetry, that was the beginning of this collection of poems.

A big thank you to all at The Society of Medical Writers (SOMW) which has been a such a helpful platform to submit writing including poetry for scrutiny and feedback. A special thanks to Dr Charmian Goldwyn at the SOMW who has been so supportive of my attempts at poetry.

My thanks to David Onyett, Rachel Woodman and everyone at The Choir Press for their support and expertise in guiding this book to publication.

Finally, thank you to my family, my sons Ben and Nathan and most of all to my wife Helen for their constant support as I journeyed through the challenges and rewards of being a family doctor. Also to my sister Liz who has been so supportive over the years and a special thanks to Ben for the cover design.

JAMES BROCKBANK

Introduction

As a physician I have been privileged to observe, and sometimes be part of, stories that reveal much about being human. I have been witness to illness, suffering, and death and I have been aware of carrying stories untold. I have wanted to articulate my experience and capture the essential reward of what it is to be a doctor.

The extraordinariness of ordinary people has been a central theme of my experience. The stories have arrived in all shapes and sizes, some are very much on the surface impatient to be heard, others need to be extracted from the deep. Cecil Helman (2006) the GP and Anthropologist, wrote that it is the stories heard in family practice, concealed behind the mask of symptoms or disease, that tell doctors the meanings that people give to their illnesses.

In 2012 I completed a masters degree in Medical Humanities. This opened the door to my understanding of how the humanities engage with and give meaning to the specific experiences of patients, doctors, health, illness and suffering. Two years later it was a retirement gift from my partners at the practice, a residential writing course, that set me on the road to writing poetry. I was also a member of The Society of Medical Writers where I could submit my poems for competitions and scrutiny which proved immensely helpful.

The great Irish poet Seamus Heaney (1995) believed that poetry allows us to contemplate the complex burden of our own experience and Dr Jack Coulehan (2005) the American poet and physician has written that poetry fosters our ability to make the leap of empathy and fully recognise our patients. I have tried to capture in word and rhythm my experience and bring a sense of meaning and recognition to what I have witnessed. The poems are not marshalled into any particular category, the stories have 'come through the door' in random order, just as patients do.

Dr Iona Heath (2011), former President of the Royal College of General Practitioners, has written that it is GPs who work at the interface between symptomatic illness and biomedical disease, where human suffering and distress meets the classification of scientific medicine. This is where the border lies and it is where these stories were found.

JAMES BROCKBANK

The Consulting Room

The knock at your door heralds
your guests who come with their
requests for remedy and counsel.

The clock on your wall marks
the years, and if they had ears
your walls would hear laughter, tears

and the hushed words of truths told,
fears revealed, and the baring
of secrets long concealed.

The view from your window
is framed with the green leaves of spring,
fading to autumnal yellow.

Herein, you and I bear witness
to the sights and sounds,
seasons and stories of sickness.

Life Force

Life force, bright colours of sound
Light up, as I pass the school playground
Spirit lifts
Young lives, vital gifts.

Make ready for the daily processional
Ebb and flow of the clinical confessional
A place of privilege in ordinary lives
Takes its toll on both sides.

He comes through the door
Defeated eyes transfixed to the floor.
Black news, white shadow, crimson cough
This telling cannot be put off.

Empathy spills across the room.
Struggle to lighten the message of doom
Fast track referral - the two week rule
Be honest. He's no fool.

Next patient please sings the digital screen
The emotional slate must wipe itself clean
Next patient please. Undercurrents remain
Cradled by the pulse of the playground refrain.

Manifesto

If you are ill, I will care for you
And pay non-judgmental attention to
Your words, newborn for my privileged ear
They carry the story that brought you here.

I will know your secrets and keep them close
Get at your illness and give a dose
Of meaning, match science with competence
To your biography and circumstance.

I will help you cope with sickness and stress
Survey your soul as well as your flesh
Drift amid distance and intimacy
Tiptoe around your autonomy.

Don't think of me as ad-hoc stranger
Let me be your compassionate neighbour
It matters not, sameness of life or hue
If you are ill, I will care for you.

Content

The light linen of her Kameez Shimmered
in the gentle breeze from an open window
as she lay on the daybed in the front room.

An Afghan flag, black red and green
fluttered on the wall. She nodded,
her son full grown fifteen, translated.

She had faced danger and uncertainty
before, widowhood and war. This time
it was cancer that ravaged her.

The doctor and nurse, shoes left at the door
would gently explore and manage her pain,
explain. She had no expectation

of being healed. What mattered most
she revealed, they were safe, had friends,
her son was doing well at school, no fool.

The doctor and nurse, excused, slipped
on their shoes and went. She smiled,
graceful, respectful, thankful. Content.

The Now and Then

He lives in the now and then
never knowing when
the scent of death and sweat
and the sights and sounds of war
will rage inside his head.

A montage of memories tripped,
baggage unzipped,
shaking, shivering,
palpitating, withering.

He reaches for the pocket torch
and gets the green light which
carries him to the here and now.
Essential oils of lavender
and bergamot calm his furrowed brow.

He's back, for now, from then
but when again
will the scent of death and sweat
and the sights and sounds of war
rage inside his head?

Lifeline

No more the garden fence routine
A beer and a bit of a moan
Now subbed for housebound lives unseen
They call through the wall on the phone.

At ninety the wartime flyer
Is grounded, immobile at home
Partitioned from friend and neighbour
He calls through the wall on the phone.

Next door, oxygen is siphoned
To gasping lungs wheezing and worn
A voice now whispered and weakened
Makes calls through the wall on the phone.

Two men cling on to the wreckage
Of old age and living alone
And hold fast to their daily dosage
Of a call through the wall on the phone.

No Tomorrow

The doctor stepped in
to the November night
and knocked at the door of sorrow.

He stepped in
to broken parents within
and stood with them in shadow.

He stepped in
to the pain of a child's life lost
and the dawn of no tomorrow.

He stepped in
to the silence of the toys,
a silence hopeless and hollow.

He stepped in
to the November night
and wept at the door of sorrow.

Rooted in duty

He's a disruptive child
he won't dress, won't eat.
He pees in the waste bin
he wanders naked in the street.

He sees phantoms and bogeymen
he's spooked and on edge.
She feels scared to be around his
paranoia and fits of rage.

He's locked her in the garage.
he follows her around.
Sometimes he doesn't know her,
sometimes he doesn't make a sound.

Rooted in duty
she's reached her limit.
*"My life is spinning by
without me in it".*

Dead on her feet
struggling to care
for the man she shared her life with.
It's more than she can bear.

A drink at lunchtime

She was a feisty Yorkshire lass
She was sassy, she had class
She had style.

He'd known her twenty years
They'd shared laughter and tears
He'd visit her once in a while.

Today he would visit
He could spare twenty minutes
He arrived at the care home in good time.

The doctor gave her a white rose
"*Happy One Hundredth Birthday*" he proposed
As they shared a glass of sparkling white wine.

If you are listening

If
You are
Listening
Recognise me
Embrace my wishes
Treat me as a person.
If I look OK to you
Don't presume that I am coping
With the changes my disease has wrought.
Make it easier to give you my name
Than to give you my hospital number.
Help me to see the achievable
Rather than the impossible.
Help me to find the courage
To face what lies ahead.
Understand my needs
Give me your time,
Go beyond
Science
Please.

The Sound of Life

It's part of the routine
He's heard it all before.
She's waited so long for this
Her tears fall to the floor.

The sound waves bounce, *and then,*
He's found it – the beat!
The doppler translates again
The sound of life, so sweet.

She gathers her composure
As from the deep it came
At double speed, the sonic roar
Of Motherhood proclaimed.

Courageous

Cancer danced into his bones
Offensive, omnipotent
Unremitting, unrepentant
Ruining, rampant
A street fight, no chance for this
Gallant gutsy combatant
Entangled, entrapped
Overthrown, overwhelmed
Unequal, unarmed
Stoical, Succumbed.

Duty Man

He
Shapes up
And shows up
When on duty
Mission crystal clear
The man for a crisis
The uniform defines him
Man of action, one of the crew
He hoists himself into the moment
And fearlessly dances amongst the flames
But in the humdrum of daily living
His dancing feet are tangled, clueless
Out of uniform, out of step
Paralysing dread-fuelled days
Halted by the jitters
Waiting to show up
And dance again
Amongst the
Blazing
Flames.

So You Want To Be a GP

So you want to be a GP
Can you live at the edge of uncertainty?
The child with a fever, the man with chest pain
It might be nothing, but there again...

Can you get the picture, the colour and shape
Of the story told and the path to take
Can you find your way if the trail isn't clear?
It can get misty and lonely up here.

Can you untangle a life that's a mess
And help someone cope with pain and distress
Can you tune in to the needy and sick?
You've six hundred seconds you'd better be quick.

Can you bear witness to body and soul
And hold the line at border control?
Can you hold your nerve, choose the right test
And make a timely referral request?

You'll deal with emergencies and chronic disease
Pregnancies, prostates and psychoses
Severe depression and suicide risk
Are you sure you're up for all of this?

Can you lead the primary care platoon
In the battle for health and call the tune
On asthma, diabetes and hypertension
The stars on the roll call of disease prevention?

Do you have an enquiring and curious mind
Can you be caring, trustful and kind
And as you spin round on the carousel
Can you look after yourself as well?

If you can do all this you're in for a treat
You'll feast on humanity and greet
Laughter and tears as you strive to do
Your best for those who trust in you.

Illusion

Starving,
A broken drunk
Stick thin, twenty kilos
Underweight, she had to lay off.
At thirty-four death was not far away
Unless she made changes, mended
Herself and found a way
To escape her
Starving.

Sixteen
When it started.
Bright, top of the class, but
Low self esteem, not good enough.
Few friends and no siblings to protect from
Bullies, her body image set
The rules, her mind held her
Illusion at
Sixteen.

Transfixed.
Preoccupied
With calorie counting.
Good at attention to detail
Top of the class in computer science
Fluent in the language and code
Of I.T. and ace at
Self destruction.
Transfixed.

Wrecking
Her self, burning
Her arms with cigarettes.
Using a joint, bingeing on booze,
The only time she felt worth anything.
She starved, fitted, overdosed see-
Sawed, no child's play here
Self destruction,
Wrecking.

Concerned
Friends clung on through
The roller coaster ride
Not sure they could go round again.
She walked off the wards and out of clinics
Hit and miss with her promises.
She was a nihilist
Saboteur, Un-
Concerned.

Hold on
Stay in control
You have won through before.
Dig deep, accept the help offered
Decode the language of self destruction
Uncouple your body image.
Mend yourself, you can be
Top of the class.
Hold on.

The Final Question

"Could you lie on the couch please"
the doctor said to the athlete.
He prodded and teased the abdomen
he was careful and complete.

Reassured of nothing untoward
but before they said goodbye
he asked "are you any good?"
"I'm the world record holder" came the reply.

The Court Report

He wakes anxious, nauseous, sweaty, early,
his skin crawls and his scary demons dance.
It begins first thing, he reaches for a can
and pulls the ring.

Six cans of eight percent cider downed by mid morning,
the snakes and rats stop dancing.
Eighteen cans later, dozens of joints, electric soup off the streets
and he's prancing about.

A twenty-five-year routine, two of them clean,
he's OD'd, fitted, sliced his wrist in between.
He's tried detox and rehab only to fail, done time in jail,
got into debt.

This time it's charges for shoplifting, carrying a knife, and assault.
The doctor sighed, not again he thought
as he prepared the court report.

Castaway

A simple sheaf of white roses given
the last act of care for a life riven
with adversity. So ill in luck and hope
that health and social care would interlope.

Castaway to a children's home
he grew up vulnerable and alone,
easy pickings self-worth shattered,
no one heard, it hadn't mattered.

And finally when he broke
he took a knife and with a stroke,
a call for help across his wrist,
his torment could not be dismissed.

Admission to a psychiatric ward
where his demons were explored
and so to clinics and to day care,
at last for him, someone was there.

But that was not all, a misspelt gene
from the family he'd never seen
grew tumours along nerves which in time
trespassed into eyes and spine.

He went to pain clinics and residential care
a host of experts gathered there
from anaesthetics and neurology
from orthopaedics and ophthalmology.

He had lived alone
in social care that he called home,
in his final months he could only see
from shape and voice who it might be.

We gathered from health and social care
in the chapel, no one else was there,
and as the service came to a close
the sunlight caught a small white rose.

Face

Alone in the darkness, curtains drawn,
Ruined flesh, wretched spirit, broken.
No teeth, no palate, no speech, no smile,
That side of his face turned towards the wall.

Dis-fig-ured, dis-owned, de-serted, dis-placed
Selfness uncoupled, image defaced.
Abject, object, alien, an *other*
Hidden in the shadows, undercover.

Coaxed into the open, a hospice place
Where carers would gaze at more than his face
And come to understand the man beneath
The mangled visage and missing teeth.

No more the biomedical gaze
The curious stares when on display
No more the shunned disgusting loner
A betting man with a sense of humour.

A day at the races, the greyhound track
And as the rivals spring from the trap
Just the trace of a smile and a thank you scrawl
A winner, one of *us*, after all.

Walter

He wore the mask of old age and distress
It was all I'd ever seen of him
Fifty years married, he missed her
Agitated and ashamed
Reluctant to seek help
Not coping alone
Frail and fearful
Widower
Tearful
Now

Then
Action
World War Two
Under cover
Resistance fighter
Strong and Intelligent
Captured, Interrogated
Courageous, escaped, his lips sealed
He had come to the point of telling
The once proud vigorous young man revealed

"I'm Just Nipping Out to the Post Office"

"I'm just nipping out to the post office"
It was part of the everyday.

She collected her stamps at the counter
There was always nothing to pay.

No letters or cards were written
No memory for things to say.

This kindly secret arrangement
Was part of the everyday.

The Cake

She gathered what remained of her self-worth
Mixed in the years of disbelief
And greased the pan with her shame.

The timer had been set in childhood
By the meddling man at the clinic ...

She heated the oven to the temperature
Of her anger and pain
And baked her cake.

She let it cool in the healing flow
Of belief and attentiveness
Before decorating in the green of renewal.

It was a gift for someone she had finally come to trust ...
Her medicine man.

Homemade Biscuits and Rhubarb

Warm hands gently worked the dough
with cold butter, baked to pale gold,
the spoils of her labour were laid
beside the thick stems, bright red
grading to dark green, that she had
tugged and twisted from the soil.

She'd been running fast for too long
couldn't keep up, got used up, and
lost her way. Seeking help, she learned
to slow down, look around,
find her own pace, create space
for a life of that *she* owned.

Gifted in a basket
for the part her doctor played,
rhubarb, and biscuits
– homemade.

The Circle of Life

She stood at the door and timidly
held out a basket of wild roses
from her garden, rich pinks, soft yellows,
crimson and red.
*"Would you like to come in
and see the new baby?"* he said.

She gently held the little pink hand,
she hadn't planned to intrude
but it lifted her mood.

"Thank you for everything doctor," she said
as she headed down the road.
It was she who made the home visit this time
the frail lady newly widowed.

As Death Came In

He journeyed into his sexuality
latent and opaque, sometimes sidetracked,
he took risks. A crisis was coming
for him, and the community of men
he knew. There was no turning back,
no hiding place for any of them.

Judgment day, the bigots would condemn them
pillory them, presume depravity.
The science wasn't smart enough back
then, an advancing army would attack
his immunity, no chance of men
-ding his body and soul, they were coming.

He slowed down, became stick thin unbecoming
reddish purple bumps on his skin, lots of them.
Kaposi's sarcoma proclaimed these men
stained them, a silent profanity.
Into his brain and lungs microbes would track,
dispatched pro tem, he knew they would be back.

He'd reached the winter of his life, back
then there was no reprieve, death was coming.
He was alone, frightened, stopped in his tracks
a long way from family, he needed them,
and his friends. No sentimentality
please. They came for him, his kinsmen.

His widowed dad, a frightened man
uncertain of what to say or do, backed
off, shaken by the brutality
of this disease. Bedbound, nurses would come in
to bathe and dress tissue thin skin, from them
he learned how to comfort his son, keep track

of his needs. Intent on helping, not sidetracked
more comfortable now, this gentle man
would clean his son's mouth with a pink sponge, then
massage oil into his shoulders and back,
and mop his brow with a tepid cloth. Combing
the thin blond hair brought tranquility.

As the microbes attacked, his dad kicked back
his shoes, and lay, mending his son. As death came in
they cradled in silent valedictory.

"Can you come over doc"

"Can you come over doc"
He called on the phone
"We've got someone,
dead at home".

"It's not a pretty sight"
The officer said at the door
The rookie beside him heaving
As 'the doc' went in to explore.

He'd been lying there for three weeks
Through the heat of June
No-one heard or saw him
As he lay in his living room.

He was dead to the world
And the world didn't care
No family no friends
The cupboard was bare.

He lived as he died
Untouched, unknown
This someone was no one, until
The officer called on the phone.

Travel Companion

Thank You for sitting with me
as I journey through the land of sickness.
Thank You for being my minder and
for bearing witness
to this dark chapter of my life.

You are an important cog
in my wheel of care.
And as I twist and turn through
the dizzying loops of hope and fear
You give me the strength to hold on.

A World Apart

He peered out from a closed world,
no one could see within.
He couldn't move a muscle,
couldn't shake a limb.

Even his breathing
passed beyond his control
too weak to shift the phlegm that chokes,
carers on patrol.

The circuitry is failing
no charge, no spark, no juice,
cruel unveiling
of muscles that are no use.

No signalling to action,
un-nerved, un-spared, un-done.
Governed by the rules of illness,
a life sentence has begun.

His breathing machine nods
in admiration and respect,
"let me know anytime
you wish to disconnect".

Heroes

Hero
Star footballer
slips into the hospice
and shoots the breeze with his young fan
Awesome
The cancer ousted by football
"Best day of my life" said
the eight-year-old
Hero

The Last Cigarette

Two
A.M.
Home visit
Woken and scared
More morphine infused
Cigarette requested
His pale cheeks hollowed, an arc
Of silver ash hung from his lips
Cautioned he might burn himself he barked
"At least I'll know that I'm effing alive".

He walked into the garage

He walked into the garage
        stepped on to the chair
        slipped the ligature
        around the beam.

    Life blown.

This teen's despair
        left hanging in mid air.

    "If only we'd known"

The Computer is King

I know you're feeling lousy
you've got the flu, while you're here
I've a few things of my own I need to do.
I have to ask about your smoking,
drinking, that sort of thing,
the computer needs the data.
The computer is King.

I know you like a cigarette,
it's important I record
I've advised you not to smoke,
even if my guidance is ignored.
If you can give up for four weeks that's the thing,
the computer will report you've quit.
The computer is King.

I know you feel miserable
and your mental health is poor,
maybe a smoke helps you cope,
but today I need to score
your asthma that's the thing,
the computer needs the data.
The computer is King.

How many days off work from asthma
have you had this week? But I forget
you don't work do you. Let's check your
inhaler technique, if you blow through the meter
we'll see what state your lungs are in,
the computer needs the data.
The computer is King.

If you reappear I'll bend the ear
of your psychiatric nurse,
let's hope in the meantime,
your mood gets no worse.
Today I need to list the risk that your lungs are in,
the computer needs the data.
The computer is King.

I hope you understand I need to catch you
while I can, get the data entered
on such an elusive man.
Maybe next time I'll ask you
what state your mind is in
but today I need the data.
The computer is King.

When the Mad House Beckoned

When the mad house beckoned
His tortured soul
She saved him.

When his ragged mind
Would daze and bemuse
She soothed him.

When the demons danced
And the devil came
She shielded him.

When the voices called
Out his name
She cradled him.

When finally the
Time came
She prayed for him.

Duty free
Tearfully
She grieved for him.

Unseeing Undone

The morning light prances
in celebration.

Halting first glances
gaze in wonder and disbelief.
Light and darkness,
joy and grief.

Swathed in your tissue so fine spun,
three lives re-cast.
Unseeing Undone.

A Walk in the Park

You are a beautiful soul
So close to our hearts

The Thames ran swiftly for you
The blossom was on the trees

Light cloud and blue skies held off the rain for you
And we walked in celebration of you.

Words From The Working Week

Pompholyx, papilloma, pregnancy, parathyroid adenoma
Tinnitus, transverse myelitis, thyroiditis, temporal arteritis,
Insomnia, IBS, immunisation, incontinence stress
Chemotherapy, cholecystitis, contraception, conjunctivitis
Dyspepsia, dysmenorrhoea, depression, dysuria
Hypertension, hyperlipidaemia, headache, heart ischaemia
Angiogram, ADHD, anterolisthesis, anxiety

Rosacea, rheumatoid arthropathy, raynaud's, radiculopathy
Medication, myelofibrosis, metastasis, multiple sclerosis
Suicide, sickle cell anaemia, seizure, schizophrenia
OCD, overdoses, organomegaly, osteoporosis
Bereavement, balanitis, benzodiazepines, bursitis
Eczema, existential neurosis, ECG, endometriosis
Neutropenia, NSAID, nocturia, neuropathy

The Clean Whipping

Slap, slap, slap on the soles of the feet,
A whipping, no durable marks, deceit.
No bones broken, nothing to expose
the well-versed beatings with a lead filled hose.

A belt or a wooden paddle will do
to contuse and bruise, no cut, no clue.
Barefoot put in water, yoghurt pasted on the feet,
discounted swelling, disguise complete.

Traces of torture disappear
but not the wretched souvenir
of jabbing, throbbing, freezing, burning,
horror, shame, and stomach churning.

Conversations

Maybe it was the skunk in your teenage years
that separated you from your self
and delivered the clamouring voices
and the demons that make your life hell.

A world we cannot see, touch, or feel
but as real as any other to you.
Do what they command, that's the deal,
your tormenters hidden from view.

Conversations, controlling words,
preying, taunting, ceaseless.
Reason and reality blurred
marooned in your broken universe.

Seeing and hearing is believing
fear and anguish consume you.
Your brain lights up, *they are coming*,
but the truth is *no one believes you.*

No hiding place, naked, violated,
you can't leave your mind and step away.
Get real, you are incarcerated,
shackled, a disconnected castaway.

Strung Out

Are you feeling on the edge,
do you have a plan?
Are you able to resist
do you think you can?

Are you feeling overwhelmed
have you tried before?
Is your pain unbearable
can't take it anymore?

Can you figure out a future
do you see one there?
Are you strung out in darkness
anguish and despair?

You tell me that you're OK
is that really true?
I may not fix things right now
but I'm here for you.

If it was my child

If it was my child,
my primal scream
would reach to the skies.
This must be a dream,
it must be lies.

I juggle with the language
of cancer as doctors explain.
I tangle with anger and guilt
Take me,
let it be my name.

I'll make a pact with
God or the Devil.
We must save her.
We're out there to kill
the malicious malignant invader.

We can win, with smart
weapons of science,
chemo in barrows
and the true flight
of our poison arrows.

I call her heroes to arms
from music, film, sport,
from anywhere.
Please comfort her.
If it was my child.

Falling Into Darkness

A dozen times daily, and more,
as your brain tears loose
you crash to the floor
and fall into darkness.
Maybe you are released
from the volcanic, tyrannic,
anarchic beast?

But this is no reverie,
this is slamming, writhing,
stigmatising savagery.
And I am lifted,
as you, unshakeable,
hold on
to your Self.

The Domestic Zoo

He'd been riding high as a kite
he couldn't slow down try as he might.
He was spending money he hadn't got
three houses, two cars and a thirty foot yacht.

A neighbour had become concerned
at bizarre behaviour, confirmed
when the holy trinity paid a call
to consider a section after all.

First a kitten then a tortoise appeared
it was all getting wonderfully weird.
A budgie flew out from behind the settee
followed by a menagerie,

a guinea pig, a rabbit, a hamster or two
no more a home, a domestic zoo.
The time had come to intercede
a mental health section was agreed.

Touch

I need you to share my pain
and touch my wounds with your
warm and tender hand.

I need you to take a moment
from your to do list
and the tests that you have planned.

I need your practised ease
to keep me calm and still,
to soften my fear, and

I need you to understand
the power
of your healing hand.

The Whipping Boy

When he was a child
his father *beat him, whipped him, sold him.*
When he was a child
the gang *beat him, worked him, stabbed him.*

When he became a man
he abandoned childish things.
But when he became a man
he could not escape his dreams.

Again, Again and Again

"I'm sorry to trouble you again doctor".

Grateful, appreciative,
flattering, exasperating,
defeating, overwhelming,
exhausting.

Letting go

You held on to yourself that morning until
you took your place in the clinical confessional.
Tears spilled down your wretched face
as the hurt burst through, surrendered to.

You chided yourself, restraint gave chase.
You delved for the image that would confide
and tendered brimful with love and pride
your daughter, a beaming mother and loving wife.

She now lay terminal, incurable.
You let go that winter morning,
grief laid bare, as you found a way to share
your defeated heart and deep distress.

Unmasked And Set Free

It took less than a moment
for the precious droplet to be installed
in my arm and give such hope that
we will not submit, we will not yield.
In time I will be unmasked and set free
to walk the world again in liberty.

This smart weapon of science
with its molecular mimicry
has made a call to arms in defiance
of you. Invade me and have no doubt
my army of B cells and T cells
will scout my body and kick you out.
And I will be unmasked and set free
to walk the world again in liberty.

Our best minds are on to you,
they have crystallised, analysed
and marked a path of destruction to
your vulnerable crown, exposed.
And I will be unmasked and set free
to walk the world again in liberty.

I have witnessed a demonstration
of the humanity of science,
of collaboration, dedication,
and the persistence of brilliant minds,
who set the bait, ensnared the foe.
Thank you. In time, because of you
I will be unmasked and set free
to walk the world again in liberty.

The regulator ruled on safety,
the manufacturer scaled up supply, the
vaccinator team made my dream come true.
Deep in gratitude, *I Thank you.*
In time I will be unmasked and set free
to walk the world again in liberty.

I must play my part, pay attention,
not out of the woods yet.
This pathogen is prone to mutation,
I will still follow the rules with respect.
Protection has come with such effort,
a mountain climbed. Now I know, in time
I will be unmasked and set free
to walk the world again in liberty.

Under the weather

*"I think it's my atmospheric pressure doctor,
but I don't really know"*

Through a barely concealed smile he asked
"are you feeling high or low?"

"I may be a little while" he said
"but I think it's something we should monitor"
as he headed off to the garden to get the barometer.

www.ingramcontent.com/pod-product-compliance
Lightning Source LLC
Chambersburg PA
CBHW022109040426
42451CB00007B/192